VIRGINIA WOOLF

Frances Lincoln Limited
74–77 White Lion Street
London N1 9PF
www.franceslincoln.com

Virginia Woolf
Copyright © Frances Lincoln Limited 2015
Text copyright © Zena Alkayat 2015
Illustration copyright © Nina Cosford 2015

First Frances Lincoln edition 2015

A catalogue record for this book is available
from the British Library.

ISBN 978-0-7112-3665-3

1 2 3 4 5 6 7 8 9

FRANCES LINCOLN LIMITED
PUBLISHERS

VIRGINIA WOOLF

by Zena Alkayat and Nina Cosford

'She sliced like a knife through everything;
at the same time was outside, looking on.'

'Mrs Dalloway', 1925

ADELINE VIRGINIA STEPHEN WAS
BORN ON 25th JANUARY 1882.
SHE GREW UP AT 22 HYDE PARK
GATE WITH HER FEROCIOUSLY
INTELLECTUAL FATHER LESLIE, HER
PHILANTHROPIC MOTHER JULIA AND
SEVEN SIBLINGS AND HALF-SIBLINGS.

LESLIE (A HISTORIAN AND CRITIC)
AND JULIA (A GREAT BEAUTY)
LOVED TO REMEMBER.

THEIR HOUSE WAS FULL OF BOOKS,
LETTERS AND MEMENTOS.

The Stephen

Herbert Duckworth

previously married

Stella
Duckworth

Gerald
Duckworth

George
Duckworth

Julia Stephen

marrie

Vanessa Stephen

Thoby Stephen

Family Tree

Harriet Stephen

previously married

married

Leslie Stephen

Laura
Stephen

Virginia Stephen

Adrian Stephen

WHILE HER BROTHERS WERE AWAY AT SCHOOL, VIRGINIA WOULD READ AND WRITE OBSESSIVELY. HER OLDER SISTER VANESSA SPENT HOURS AT HER EASEL.

THEY WENT ON TO DEVOTE THEIR LIVES TO EACH OTHER.

HAPPIEST DURING FAMILY HOLIDAYS
TO TALLAND HOUSE IN ST IVES,
VIRGINIA ADORED PLAYING CRICKET AND
WAS AN ACE BOWLER. SHE ALSO LOVED
TO LISTEN TO THE WAVES BREAKING
- ONE TWO, ONE TWO -
AND TAKE LONG COASTAL WALKS
WITH HER FATHER.

HER CONTENTED CHILDHOOD
WAS CUT SHORT WHEN HER
MOTHER DIED. VIRGINIA WAS 13
YEARS OLD AND HEARTBROKEN.

THE DEATH OF HER HALF-SISTER
STELLA FOLLOWED IN 1897.
HER FATHER PASSED AWAY
IN FEBRUARY 1904.

INCONSOLABLE, VIRGINIA WAS
CONSIGNED TO BED FOR MONTHS.
SHE REFUSED TO EAT AND HEARD
BIRDS SINGING IN GREEK.

AFTER LESLIE'S DEATH,
VANESSA PACKED UP THE FAMILY
HOME ALONG WITH ALL ITS
HISTORY. THE STEPHENS WERE
TO MAKE A FRESH START AT
46 GORDON SQUARE, BLOOMSBURY.

'All the voices I used to hear
telling me to do all kinds of
wild things have gone.'

Letter, September 1904

ON THURSDAY EVENINGS,
VIRGINIA'S BROTHER THOBY WOULD
INVITE HIS CAMBRIDGE FRIENDS TO
GATHER IN THE PARLOUR TO DISCUSS
ART, POLITICS, PHILOSOPHY AND
THEIR GRAND IDEAS.

THIS WAS THE START OF THE
BOHEMIAN 'BLOOMSBURY GROUP',
AND VIRGINIA DELIGHTED IN
HER NEW FREEDOM.

OVER THE YEARS, THE NEBULOUS
BLOOMSBURY GROUP BECAME
SHORTHAND FOR AN UNCONVENTIONAL
AND NON-CONFORMIST SET
OF FRIENDS.

THE BLOC

THE WRITERS

Lytton
Strachey

Virginia
Woolf

E.M.
Forster

THE THINKERS

Saxon
Sydney-Turner

Leonard
Woolf

...NSBURYS

Clive
Bell

THE ARTISTS

Duncan
Grant

Vanessa
Bell

Roger
Fry

THE ECONOMIST

John Maynard Keynes

THE MOVE TO GORDON SQUARE
ALSO GAVE VIRGINIA A ROOM
OF HER OWN. SHE BEGAN
REVIEWING BOOKS, WRITING
ESSAYS AND ARTICLES, AND
BUILDING A REPUTATION AS
A FORMIDABLE CRITIC.

'Do you think i shall ever write
a really good book?'

Letter, October 1905

VIRGINIA TOOK TO
'STREET HAUNTING'. SHE RAMBLED
THROUGH BLOOMSBURY TO
WATCH PASSERS-BY, OVERHEAR
CONVERSATIONS AND SPECULATE
ABOUT THE GOINGS-ON
BEHIND LAMPLIT WINDOWS.

SHE WOULD WALK VANESSA'S
SHEEPDOG GURTH.

LIFE WOULD NOT REMAIN
SO SPIRITED. BELOVED THOBY
DIED IN 1906. VANESSA MARRIED HIS
FRIEND CLIVE BELL THE FOLLOWING
YEAR, OBLIGING VIRGINIA AND HER
BROTHER ADRIAN TO MOVE A SHORT
WALK AWAY TO 29 FITZROY SQUARE.

DUNCAN GRANT, MAYNARD KEYNES AND ROGER FRY LIVED NEARBY, AND THE BLOOMSBURY GROUP MEETINGS CONTINUED.

TIMES WERE CHANGING...
THE SUFFRAGE MOVEMENT WAS
IN FULL SWING AND THERE WAS
A NEW OPENNESS AMONG
THE FRIENDS TO TALK ABOUT SEX
AND SEXUALITY. THE BLOOMSBURY
GROUP WAS PRODUCING AVANT-GARDE
WORK AND FORGING A NEW
WAY TO LIVE.

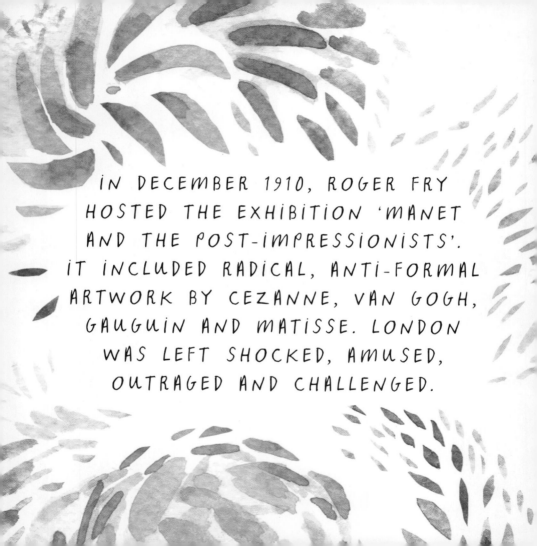

IN DECEMBER 1910, ROGER FRY HOSTED THE EXHIBITION 'MANET AND THE POST-IMPRESSIONISTS'. IT INCLUDED RADICAL, ANTI-FORMAL ARTWORK BY CEZANNE, VAN GOGH, GAUGUIN AND MATISSE. LONDON WAS LEFT SHOCKED, AMUSED, OUTRAGED AND CHALLENGED.

'On or about December 1910,
human character changed.'

Essay, 1924

AMIDST THE FUSION OF LIBERAL LIVING AND POLITE EDWARDIAN SOCIETY, VANESSA AND CLIVE HAD TWO CHILDREN.

VANESSA WAS A NATURAL MOTHER, JUST LIKE JULIA BEFORE HER.

Quentin

Julian

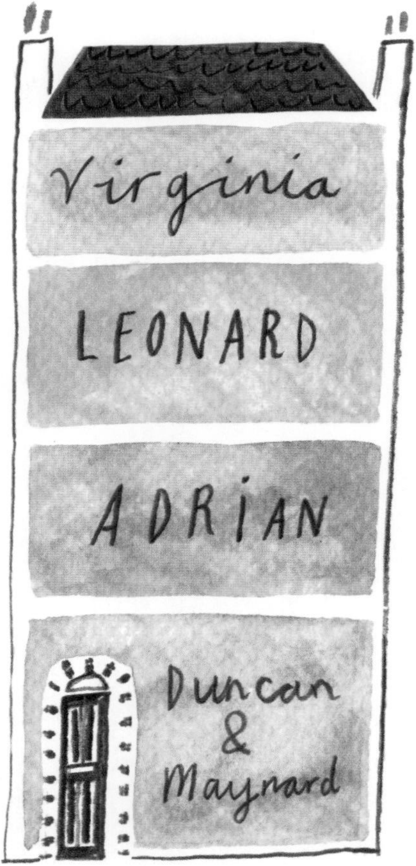
Virginia
LEONARD
ADRIAN
Duncan
&
Maynard

VIRGINIA AND ADRIAN MOVED TO
38 BRUNSWICK SQUARE IN 1911
AND CONCEIVED A COMMUNAL
LIVING PLAN WHICH SAW VIRGINIA
SCANDALOUSLY SHARING A HOUSE
WITH FOUR MEN: HER BROTHER
AND THEIR FRIENDS DUNCAN
AND MAYNARD, AS WELL AS
LEONARD WOOLF.

VIRGINIA DREW UP LEONARD'S
TENANCY AGREEMENT.

'Meals are:

Breakfast 9 a.m.
Lunch   1.
Tea   4.30 p.m.
Dinner   8 p.m.

Trays will be placed
in the hall punctually
at these hours.'

LEONARD HAD SPENT SEVEN YEARS
WORKING FOR THE COLONIAL
CIVIL SERVICE IN CEYLON. HE WAS
A WRITER, AN INTELLECTUAL
AND A PERFECTIONIST.

HE WAS ALSO TALL AND
DARK WITH BLUE EYES AND
TREMBLING HANDS.

Leonard Woolf

IN JANUARY 1912, LEONARD
ASKED VIRGINIA TO MARRY HIM.
MONTHS OF COURTSHIP ENSUED,
BUT SHE WAS UNSURE ABOUT THEIR
FUTURE HAPPINESS AND KEPT HIM
WAITING FOR AN ANSWER. THEY
WERE EVENTUALLY MARRIED
ON 10th AUGUST.

VIRGINIA WAS 30, LEONARD WAS 31.

LEONARD WOULD CALL HER 'MANDRILL'

VIRGINIA WOULD CALL HIM 'MONGOOSE'

A BEAUTY LIKE HER MOTHER, VIRGINIA ALSO LOOKED RATHER ECCENTRIC. HER HAIR PINS OFTEN FELL LOOSE AND SHE WAS SELF-CONSCIOUS ABOUT DRESSING UP.

VIRGINIA'S HONEYMOON WAS SHARPLY FOLLOWED BY A PERIOD OF ILLNESS. THE SUMMER OF 1913 SAW HER STRUGGLING UNDER THE STRAIN OF CORRECTING PROOFS FOR HER DEBUT NOVEL 'THE VOYAGE OUT'. SHE WAS ON THE BRINK OF A BREAKDOWN.

DOCTORS WERE CONSULTED, REST WAS PRESCRIBED. BUT IN SEPTEMBER, SHE TOOK AN OVERDOSE OF SLEEPING DRUGS.

ON THE EVE OF WORLD WAR ONE, AND DURING A BRIEF RESPITE FROM HER ILLNESS, VIRGINIA AND LEONARD MOVED TO HOGARTH HOUSE IN THE LONDON SUBURB OF RICHMOND. BUT SHE SUFFERED A RELAPSE JUST AS 'THE VOYAGE OUT' WAS PUBLISHED.

IT TOOK 15 YEARS TO SELL 2,000 COPIES.

BY 1916, SHE WAS OUT OF THE WOODS, AND SLOWLY BEGAN TO WORK. AGAINST A BACKDROP OF WAR, SHE WROTE 'NIGHT AND DAY' (1919). AND IN THE FOLLOWING DECADE, SHE BEGAN 'JACOB'S ROOM' (1922).

THE FIRST WAS DEEMED A GENTLY
SUBVERSIVE NOVEL OF MANNERS,
THE SECOND AN EXPERIMENTAL,
ELEGIAC STORY OF A YOUNG MAN.

MEANWHILE, VANESSA (NOW SEPARATED FROM CLIVE BELL) ABANDONED LONDON AND LEFT FOR SUSSEX. SHE MOVED TO A CHARMING, REMOTE COTTAGE CALLED CHARLESTON.

WITH HER CAME HER CHILDREN JULIAN AND QUENTIN, AS WELL AS CONSCIENTIOUS OBJECTOR DUNCAN GRANT AND HIS LOVER DAVID 'BUNNY' GARNETT.

Charleston

AS THE WAR RAGED ON, VIRGINIA AND LEONARD SPENT MANY NIGHTS SITTING ON BOXES UNDER SHELTER IN THE COAL CELLAR.

IN 1917 VIRGINIA AND LEONARD
SPLASHED OUT ON A PRINTING PRESS.
THEY NAMED THEIR NEW PUBLISHING
VENTURE AFTER THEIR RICHMOND
HOME 'HOGARTH' AND BEGAN THE
TRICKY PROCESS OF LEARNING
TO PRINT BOOKS.

VANESSA DESIGNED BOOK JACKETS,
FRIENDS WERE INVITED TO WRITE
FOR THE PRESS, AND OVER THE
YEARS, PUBLISHED AUTHORS
INCLUDED E.M. FORSTER, T.S. ELIOT
AND KATHERINE MANSFIELD.

'The days melted into each other like
snowballs roasting in the sun.'

Diary, March 1918

ON A VISIT TO CHARLESTON,
VANESSA CONFESSED TO VIRGINIA
SHE WAS EXPECTING A BABY, AND
THAT IT WAS DUNCAN GRANT'S.

ANGELIC BELL WAS BORN JUST AFTER
WORLD WAR ONE IN DECEMBER 1918.
SHE WAS 18 BEFORE SHE DISCOVERED
DUNCAN, NOT CLIVE, WAS HER
REAL FATHER.

IN 1919, VIRGINIA AND LEONARD
BOUGHT A SUMMER COTTAGE NEAR
CHARLESTON IN RODMELL.

Monk's House

'Monk's House... will be our address for ever and ever; Indeed I've already marked out our graves in the yard which joins our meadow.'

Letter, August 1919

IT WAS CHARLESTON, THOUGH,
THAT THE BLOOMSBURY GROUP MADE
THEIR RETREAT. IT WAS DECORATED
ENTHUSIASTICALLY BY VANESSA
AND DUNCAN, WITH MURALS ON
THE WALLS, PAINTED FURNITURE
AND A CHAOS OF COLOUR.

THERE WAS A TRANQUIL WALLED GARDEN, AS WELL AS STUDIES, STUDIOS AND SPARE ROOMS FOR THE BLOOMSBURY GUESTS.

IN VIRGINIA'S EYES, VANESSA'S
LIFE WAS FULL OF EXCITEMENT,
LOVE AFFAIRS, DEVOTED
MOTHERHOOD, TRAVEL, ART
AND ADVENTURE.

VIRGINIA LONGED TO LEAVE
RICHMOND AND TO BE BACK IN
THE 'SIZZLE' OF LONDON, WHERE
SHE COULD WANDER THROUGH
THE STREETS, GO TO MUSEUMS,
GALLERIES AND CONCERTS,
AND 'GO ADVENTURING
AMONG HUMAN BEINGS'.

IN 1924, SHE WON LEONARD OVER
(HE WAS INITIALLY CONCERNED
LONDON MIGHT OVEREXCITE HER)
AND THEY MOVED TO 52 TAVISTOCK
SQUARE, BLOOMSBURY.

IT WAS LATER BOMBED AND
DESTROYED IN WORLD WAR TWO.

WHETHER THEY WERE IN LONDON OR SUSSEX, LEONARD AND VIRGINIA INDULGED A SWEET TOOTH.

DESPITE HER GROWING FAME AS
A CRITIC AND ESSAYIST, VIRGINIA
WAS REACHING FOR SOMETHING
NEW THROUGH FICTION, FOR RADICAL
POSSIBILITIES IN LITERATURE.

'There's no doubt
in my mind that I have
found out how to begin
(at 40) to say something
in my own voice.'

Diary, july 1922

Virginia

photo of
Julia

reading glasses

sweets

potted
plant

pen pot

manuscript

s Desk

water
jug

oil lamp

diary

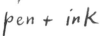
pen + ink

hairgrips

lamp from
Vanessa

'MRS DALLOWAY' - AN AMBITIOUS,
ADVENTUROUS EXPERIMENT
IN FORM - WAS PUBLISHED IN 1925.
FICTION WAS NEVER THE SAME AGAIN.

'I will not be "famous" "great".
I will go on adventuring, changing,
opening my mind and my eyes, refusing
to be stamped and stereotyped.'

Diary, October 1933

WHILE ENJOYING LONDON'S PARTY SCENE, VIRGINIA MET THE ARISTOCRATIC VITA SACKVILLE-WEST.

VITA'S LIFE WAS SCANDALOUS: SHE HAD AN OPEN MARRIAGE, PASSIONATE LESBIAN AFFAIRS AND A PENCHANT FOR CROSS-DRESSING. SHE WAS ALSO A MOTHER, A WRITER AND A POET.

AS THEIR RELATIONSHIP BUBBLED
AND FIZZED, VIRGINIA WROTE
'TO THE LIGHTHOUSE'. IT WAS
AN ODE TO HER PARENTS.

FOLLOWING ITS SUCCESS IN 1927,
SHE AND LEONARD BOUGHT A CAR.

THEY NAMED IT 'THE UMBRELLA'.

VIRGINIA QUICKLY FOLLOWED
WITH 'ORLANDO'. IT WAS A WILD,
SATIRICAL ROMP AND A FANTASTICAL
FUSION OF HISTORY AND BIOGRAPHY.
ITS SEX-CHANGING TITLE CHARACTER
MOVED FROM COUNTRY TO COUNTRY
OVER 300 YEARS.

IT WAS A TRIBUTE TO VITA.

'Nothing thicker than a knife's blade
separates happiness from melancholy.'

'Orlando', 1928

'MRS DALLOWAY' PAID FOR A NEW BATHROOM TO BE INSTALLED AT MONK'S HOUSE; 'ORLANDO' PAID FOR VIRGINIA'S NEW BEDROOM.

WHILE WORKING ON 'A ROOM OF ONE'S OWN' (A PROVOCATIVE ESSAY ON WOMEN'S PLACE IN MALE-DOMINATED LITERARY HISTORY) VIRGINIA BUILT A WRITING ROOM FOR HERSELF AT THE END OF THE GARDEN AT MONK'S HOUSE.

Hans

Grizzle

Pinka   Sally

OVER THE YEARS, VIRGINIA HAD
VARIOUS DOGS, INCLUDING HANS
(WHO HAD TROUBLE WITH HOUSE
RULES), A MONGREL FOX-TERRIER
NAMED GRIZZLE, A COCKER SPANIEL
NAMED PINKA AND A SECOND
SPANIEL CALLED SALLY.

LEONARD HAD A PET MARMOSET.

MITZ WENT EVERYWHERE WITH THEM, DELIGHTING SOME FRIENDS AND DISTURBING OTHERS.

'THE WAVES' WAS PUBLISHED IN 1931. IT WAS A POETIC MEDITATION ON THE INNER VOICE FOLLOWING SIX FRIENDS OVER A LIFETIME.

IT WAS VIRGINIA'S
EXPERIMENT WITH RHYTHM IN
PLACE OF PLOT, AND A HOMAGE TO
HER BLOOMSBURY CLIQUE.

VIRGINIA WRANGLED
PAINFULLY WITH HER NEXT NOVEL,
'THE YEARS' (IT TOOK FIVE YEARS
TO WRITE AND WAS PUBLISHED IN
1937). IT SOLD 43,909 COPIES IN
THE FIRST SIX MONTHS.

LUCKILY, MONK'S HOUSE
CONTINUED TO OFFER A PEACEFUL
RETREAT. VIRGINIA WAS A TERRIFIC
BOWLS PLAYER AND LEONARD LOVED
TO POTTER IN THE GARDEN.

Basil

Cardamom

Tomato plant

Sage

coriander

conifer

Rosemary

chilli pepper

Lime tree

Hyacinth

Thyme

Geranium

chives

Lavender

Mint

Bay Tree

AS EVER, DEATH OCCUPIED VIRGINIA'S THOUGHTS AS WELL AS HER LIFE. SHE LOST CLOSE FRIEND LYTTON STRACHEY IN 1932, HER HERO ROGER FRY PASSED AWAY IN 1934, AND HER NEPHEW JULIAN WAS TRAGICALLY KILLED IN JULY 1937 WHEN HE JOINED THE FIGHT AGAINST FASCISM IN THE SPANISH CIVIL WAR.

IT WAS NOW VIRGINIA'S TURN
TO SUPPORT VANESSA, AND SHE
MADE DAILY VISITS TO CHARLESTON.
BUT HORROR LOOMED AGAIN,
AND SHE WAS SOON SEWING
BLACKOUT CURTAINS.

THE PRIME MINISTER ANNOUNCED
THE COUNTRY WAS AT WAR WITH
GERMANY ON 3rd SEPTEMBER 1939.

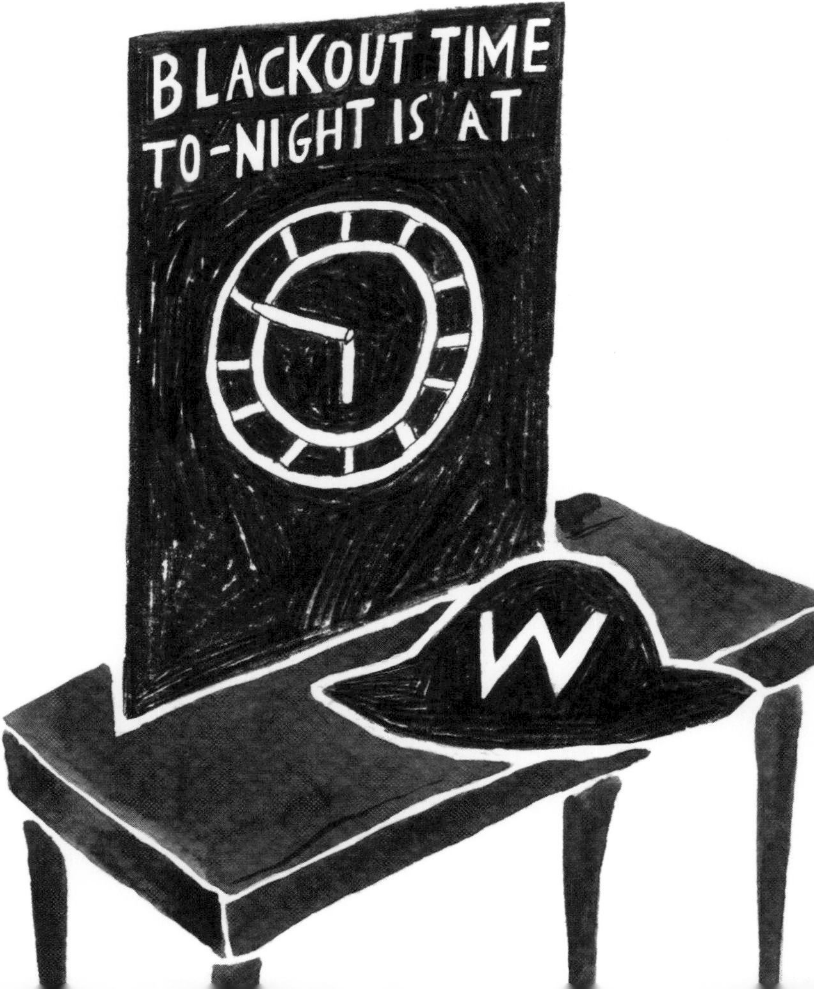
BLACKOUT TIME
TO-NIGHT IS AT
W

A GRIM VERSION OF LIFE CONTINUED AS HITLER ADVANCED THROUGH EUROPE. BRITAIN WAS CONSTANTLY SUBJECT TO HIS SPEECHES ON THE RADIO AND THE ROAR OF GERMAN BOMBERS OVERHEAD.

VIRGINIA WAS BECOMING
DESPONDENT. SHE STARTED WORK
ON 'BETWEEN THE ACTS',
BUT ON FINISHING FELT IT
WAS 'SILLY AND TRIVIAL'.

THE NOVEL (ABOUT A PLAY
MOUNTED IN AN ENGLISH
VILLAGE) WOULD BE PUBLISHED
POSTHUMOUSLY.

'Books are the mirrors of the soul.'

Between the Acts, 1941

'I am doing what seems the best thing to do. You have given me the greatest possible happiness... I don't think two people could have been happier... I can't go on spoiling your life any longer.'

Letter, March 1941

ON THE MORNING OF 28th MARCH 1941, VIRGINIA PUT ON A FUR COAT, PICKED UP HER STICK AND WENT OUT TO THE RIVER OUSE.

SHE COLLECTED HEAVY STONES AND
DROPPED THEM IN HER POCKETS.
SHE WAS 59.

LEONARD BURIED VIRGINIA'S ASHES
IN THE GARDEN AT MONK'S HOUSE
BENEATH THE ELM TREES THEY
HAD NAMED AFTER THEMSELVES.

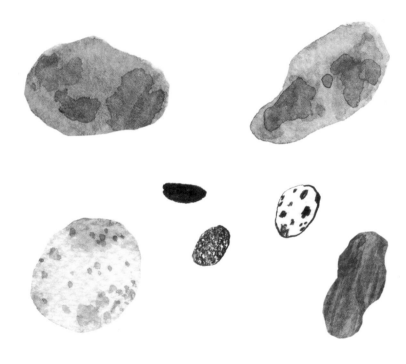

Acknowledgements

The author would like to gratefully acknowledge in particular the information and inspiration provided by Hermione Lee´s *Virginia Woolf*. Lee´s biography is not only a definitive account of the life of one of the twentieth century´s greatest authors, but is also moving, evocative and generous in its approach. Additionally, the author would like to acknowledge *Virginia Woolf* by Alexandra Harris – a celebratory biography that is as sensitive as it is revealing. Further thanks go to the Society of Authors, The Random House Group and Houghton Mifflin Harcourt Publishing Company for assisting with the use of material in copyright.

The illustrator would like to extend her love and thanks to Ali, Ma, Pops, Jojo and Chester.